What people are saying about the ministry of Steve Riggle...

For the believer, redefinition of commonly used terms is necessary. For followers of Jesus, "sharp" doesn't mean "clever" but *penetrating;* living "on the edge" doesn't mean "out in left field" but *at the swordpoint of God's Word* as it shapes your life and advances Jesus' Kingdom purposes through you. That is what this book is about–the *real* meaning of these terms; and I know of no more *real* pastor in America than Steve Riggle.

–Jack W. Hayford, Founding Pastor/Chancellor, The Church On The Way, The King's College & Seminary, Van Nuys, California

If ever an author and a book title "fit," it is this book. Steve Riggle IS "the sharper edge." Everything he does has purpose, focus and class. I have sought his counsel on many occasions. And why do I keep going back to him for advice? Succinctly, he has "the sharper edge." Anything by Steve Riggle is "must" reading!

–Jim Garlow, Senior Pastor, Skyline Wesleyan Church, La Mesa, California

There are many voices in the world today. Many significant. Some that go beyond significance; they are standards by which new parameters are set. Steve Riggle is such a voice. He is one of the truly great leaders whose voice rises to the surface of contemporary Christianity, yet he still holds the historical values that are the pillars upon which truth is established, his history shaped his future. Today Steve Riggle pastors one of the greatest churches in America, directing a cutting-edge fellowship of ministries, setting a pace to change our futures. *The Sharper*

Edge by Steve Riggle lives up to its title. It slices through the mundane to the material. He has set the sharp, cutting truth deep into the icy formations of cynical America with amazing clarity.
  –Dave Roever, Roever Evangelistic Association, Fort Worth, Texas

Steve Riggle is a gifted leader with a passion for the Church and the city. His integrity and competence have catapulted him to a place of significant leadership for the Church in the Houston area. He is a man of faith who takes risks for the sake of the Kingdom, and God is using him in clear and compelling ways to mobilize the Church in the city. Despite his obvious influence, he is a man of deep humility with a servant's heart.
  –Jim Herrington, Mission Houston

Steve Riggle is a uniquely gifted leader whose influence is far-reaching. His ministry exceeds the immediate realm of his local church and the group of churches who look to him for leadership. His years of experience and practical application of kingdom principles impact those who know him. Steve brings the heart of a shepherd and the business expertise of a CEO into the city and communities that he serves. A humble-spirited man who walks in the confidence of the Lord, he has earned the respect of his peers and colleagues. A wise counselor and friend, my life has been challenged and encouraged through our years of friendship. Steve is a strong and stable pillar in the church community who causes people to want to associate with him. Truly I can say of Steve Riggle that he is a man who lives by the principles that he upholds to those around him. A man of character and commitment, Steve's message will impact your life as it has mine.
  –Doug Stringer, Founder, Somebody Cares, Houston

THE SHARPER EDGE

Uncommon Sense for the
Journey of Life

THE SHARPER EDGE

Uncommon Sense for the
Journey of Life

A "Living On The Edge" Series

by STEVE RIGGLE

watercolor books®
Southlake, Texas

The Sharper Edge

ISBN 1-931682-09-7

Pastor Steve Riggle
Grace Community Church
P. O. Box 891409
Houston, TX 77289-1409
www.gracecchouston.org

Published by Watercolor Books®
P. O. Box 93234
Southlake, TX 76092
www.watercolorbooks.com

DEDICATION

I dedicate this book to my family.

First, to my parents who taught me to live the way of the Lord.

To Becky, our thirty-two years together have been more than I could ever have hoped for. Thank you for believing in me when I didn't.

To Cheri & Jared, Rachele and Scott, my daughters and sons-in-law. Thanks for all your love and support.

To my grandchildren, Blake, Madison, Conner, and Rebecca Lynn, who are the joy of my life. As my friend Dave Roever says– Grandchildren are the reward for not killing your own.

ACKNOWLEDGEMENTS

Special thanks to my friend Doug Stringer who has continually encouraged me to begin writing.

To Tami Barbour, my assistant, for the unselfish giving of yourself to work on this project.

To Joann Webster–without your skill and dedication this book would never be a reality.

TABLE OF CONTENTS

Winning in most cases is calculated by an edge.

"But what things were gain to me, these
I have counted loss for
Christ...that I may gain Christ."
Phil 3:7-8

ONE

LIFE ON THE EDGE

The Alpine racer's gold helmet flashed across the finish line as he conquered the mountain, shushed to stop, and jerked off his goggles to check his time. Spectators roared as the clock gave him the lead by one one-hundredth of a second. His skiing was over, but his heart kept racing as he watched each competitor try to beat his time. Finally the last racer charged the slope, coming up one-tenth of a second short. The gold medal belonged to the gold-helmeted skier.

After the race, an interviewer asked about his technique.

"The technique was to ski fast," he said, "it was my edges that won."

"You attribute the win to your edges?"

"I set my edges and just ski with reckless abandon."

Getting an "edge" takes many forms. Avid skiers know that beveling the edges on skis lifts the bottom off the snow, creating speed and facilitating turns. In the fastest non-motorized sport on earth, Alpine skiers depend on equipment engineering as much as personal training and practice. Thousands of dollars and man hours are expended to find the right relationship between the base and side edge bevels for each race, depending on conditions such as incline and iciness. Ending with a gold medal or no medal depends on whether you can trust your edge.

I will never know the "edge" of the Alpine skier, but I do remember the first time we went skiing in the Colorado Mountains. A dozen of us who had never skied before managed to knock the whole class off their feet before we ever made it to the bunny slopes. After a couple of hours of instruction and the assurance of our instructor that we really could get off the lift at the top of the beginner slope, she sent us out with instructions to wait at the top for her. (I really think she was trying to get rid of us.) We all somehow managed to get off the lift though it was anything but graceful. We found our way to each other and held on to one another wondering how in the world we were going to make it down the hill. We immediately discovered that the snowplowing technique doesn't work if you really want to stop.

All of a sudden my friend, Andy–known to do crazy things–took off down the hill, went from one side of the run to the other and crashed into the trees at the edge of the slope. Unable to move, we watched, wondering why he left the class and took off all by himself. When the instructor came and we made it down to Andy, we said, "Why did you take off all by yourself?"

"I didn't take off all by myself," he said. "My skis took off and I couldn't stop!"

You can tell none of us, including Andy, had experience with the "edge" that could help us turn or stop as we made our way down the mountain. The only sense of abandon we knew was the sheer panic of being totally out of control.

Winning in most cases is calculated by an edge. Life or death often hangs on an edge. The Space Shuttle Challenger exploded because the edge of one seal didn't fit. People's lives were lost, an entire industry jeopardized, school children traumatized, and a nation mourned because of an o-ring measured in microns.

Life, success, leadership are all about edges. Are you leading or following? Making progress or falling back?

Having a sharpened edge is crucial to win, to lead others

and, as Christians, to edge out our greatest opponent in life, the devil. The subtle deception of the enemy of our soul is to get us to live with less than a "sharpened edge" to our lives. Sharpening our edge means reaching a purposed destination, and getting there God's way.

We have a purpose, a destination that God has ordained for us, that caused us to be born and live right now in this generation and this area. Whether we achieve that purpose, and whether we do it God's way, is dependent upon whether we rely on our own abilities and devices or depend on God's.

As God's children, and His ambassadors in this earth, our edges are many and varied. How we handle life's edgy areas–ethics, finances, prayer life, personal spiritual growth, heart, appetite to know God–determines how successful we are in life's race. The environment you fashion out of your thoughts, your beliefs, your ideals, your philosophy is the only climate you will ever live in.[1] We can really live by experiencing God joining His supernatural power with our human ability. God moves on our behalf as we allow Him to focus our lives and sharpen our edge. We can set our edges, then thrust ourselves God-ward with reckless abandon.

The opportunity of a
lifetime must be
seized during the lifetime
of the opportunity.

"The night is coming when no one can work."
John 9:4

TWO

EDGE OF TIME

Why sharpen our edge? Because if we have a heart to make our lives count, we have to remember that time won't stand still for us. Paraphrasing the Apostle Paul, "forgetting those things that are behind and reaching for the future."[1] This is the essence of leadership. The leader, the vision caster, must see and foresee–to see the needs and practical directives for the present, to foresee the future with the Holy Spirit focus on what God wills in the largeness of His ordained purpose for me and for His ministry through me.

We never know how long a present window of opportunity will remain open, which will affect our future. A popular saying today is, "The opportunity of a lifetime must be seized during the lifetime of the opportunity." These words speak volumes about what I call "destiny moments" in our lives. The interesting thing about God's destiny moments is that they rarely come at ideal times. When you study the life of Jesus, He rarely performed a scheduled miracle. Miracles and healings almost always seemed as if they were interruptions to His schedule.

In our lives, the Lord brings us to many crossroads where, in a moment of time, we must choose our own human reasoning or respond to what He is speaking to our hearts. My experience is that God's timing seems opposite to what human logic says is ideal.

One of Solomon's greatest pearls of wisdom dealt with timing: "He who observes the wind will not sow, And he who regards the clouds will not reap. As you do not know what is the way of the wind, Or how the bones grow in the womb of her who is with child, So you do not know the works of God who makes everything. In the morning sow your seed, And in the evening do not withhold your hand; For you do not know which will prosper, Either this or that, Or whether both alike will be good."[2] Eccl 11:4-6

We find plenty of reasons to withhold, stay safe, await a better time, when we "watch the wind." God's timing is not dependent on circumstances–neither famine nor blessing. But if human logic and circumstances serve as our criteria for the "ideal" time, the enemy will always see to it that we miss opportunities in favor of a "better" time.

We arrive at God's timing by considering the need, examining the motives of our heart, and listening to the voice of His Spirit within us. If we consider anything other than this, we will always find reason not to sow.

I live in Texas, home to some colorful characters including billionaire Presidential candidate Ross Perot. In his years of business and team-building, Perot has observed, "Most people give up just when they're about to achieve success. They quit on the one yard line. They give up at the last minute of the game, one foot from a winning touchdown."

What football fan will ever forget NFL television anchor John Madden recommending the Patriots settle for a tie in Superbowl XXXVI, only to watch Coach Bill Belichick set up a game-winning field goal with kicker Adam Vinatieri in the last seconds of the game? That's living on the edge of time.

In Christianity, I'm convinced most people go only so far and then stop because they begin to depend on their own logic and timing. What begins as a faith walk–trusting God to meet our needs–becomes an unwillingness to risk for fear of losing whatever we've gained. People in business do the same. Our success can become our biggest liability. For fear of losing what we've gained we can become unwilling to risk again in order to advance and grow.

The patriarch Isaac came to a crossroads in his life. A famine in the land left him with only three choices:

(1) Go to Egypt

(2) Stay and ration his seed until he ate it all

(3) Sow by faith in the Word of God

God spoke to Isaac saying, "stay and occupy this land." So Isaac sowed in that land in the middle of a famine and received that same year a hundred-fold harvest and the Lord's great blessing.[3]

Circumstances would have told him to go to Egypt. Human logic would have dictated, "If you are not going to Egypt, at least save the seed you have so you can eat. Maybe you'll make it through the famine." That's how we think. When we don't seem to have enough–we can hoard or we can sow. What we hoard will last a little while. What we sow will last forever because God still honors faith, and faith puts us on life's sharpest edge.

Out of one of those edge moments my wife Becky wrote the following:

Not long ago I found myself at that place in life I call "The Edge."

I looked out to my left and over to my right trying to find a place to run, but nothing was in sight.

So I chose to take the step and He was there; all my needs were met.

But that was last time and now I stand, once again on that oh so dreaded land.

It's a new thing now that I face and I must again step out in faith,

For I know from the edge of the past He'll be there to help me through this task.

The edge memories are precious stories. They renew my faith, encourage others, and give Him glory.

I must go on–new mountains to climb. And I'm sure there will be another "edge" in time.

Where in your life is God speaking to you to quit watching the wind? Where does God want to enlarge and stretch you? Where are you waiting for a "better" moment to sow? Where does God want to use you that you've been unwilling to go?

God's destiny moments for you are directly tied to your willingness to obey what He speaks to your heart. We live in a day and age that is not just a time to survive, but to move past the limitations of our fears and human reasoning to hear the heart and intent of the One who called us and empowered us, and who challenges us to trust Him in our "opportunity of a lifetime." These are the moments when God offers the opportunity of a risk of faith–a chance to leap to more effective ministry or business, or to draw back to safe mediocrity.

Remember, in this one life over which we are stewards, God has given us exactly twenty-four hours in each day. We choose to maximize those hours by preparing our hearts to hear and obey God, or to minimize those hours by playing it safe and avoiding risk. We will only live a life with no regrets if we sharpen ourselves to take advantage of the edge of time. Someone said, "You will maximize your potential when you are willing to give up at any moment all that you are, to receive all that you can be."

If you're not
living on the edge,
you're
taking up too
much space.

"But this He said to test him, for
He Himself knew what He would do."
John 6:6

THREE

VIEW FROM THE EDGE

"If you're not living on the edge, you're taking up too much space." That's a favorite saying of my friend Jackson Senyonga. What is the difference between people who take up space and those who cut a sharp edge through life? For the Christian, "sharpening our edge" trumpets a challenge. We have to ask, will the full purpose and potential of our lives be lived out or will we become victims of a mere "existence" mindset and, because of it, live in mediocrity? There's room for every Christian to make a difference in his or her world. One major distinction between people who live on the edge and those who maintain the status quo lies in the ability to see what others miss.

For example, notice the responses of the people involved in this familiar Bible passage:

"Then Jesus lifted up His eyes, and seeing a great multitude coming toward Him, He said to Philip, 'Where shall we buy bread, that these may eat?' But this He said to test him, for He Himself knew what He would do. Philip answered Him, 'Two hundred denarii worth of bread is not sufficient for them, that every one of them may have a little.' One of His disciples, Andrew, Simon Peter's brother, said to Him, 'There is a lad here who has five barley loaves and two small fish, but what are they among so many?' Jesus then took the loaves and fishes, blessed them, then broke them into miraculous pieces that fed the entire crowd."[1]

Who in this story had the sharpest edge? Certainly not Philip, who saw a need so vast that there was "no way" they could do anything about it. Andrew was a bit sharper because at least he looked around to see what was directly on hand, even though he concluded that they could do very little. His words are akin to, "We can only do what we can do."

What Jesus was looking for from His disciples was a response of, "We don't know Lord, but You do–all things are possible with You." In this moment of challenge Jesus takes them past the edge of human possibility that they might see God's possibility.

Jesus had the edge we desire and need. He saw that the need required supernatural provision and that God was on hand to supply every need. That kind of "seeing" meant that five loaves and two small fish could become a satisfying meal for thousands of very hungry people.

Always occupying the cutting edge, Jesus looked to the Father for His solutions and actions and words. In our lives, it is imperative we follow Christ's example, looking to the Father for fresh perspective. It is critical that we move past our limited understanding of things around us and lift up our heads to see what God sees in our peculiar circumstances. Whatever our situation, we can be sure people nearby are hoping someone can look at impossibilities from God's point of view and make a difference.

The Christian stateswoman Susan B. Anthony wrote, "O, Slavery, hateful thing that thou art thus to blunt the keen edge of conscience." Hundreds of thousands of slaves at one time in America were waiting for somebody–anybody–to have an "edge of conscience" that would compel them to bring an end to the travesty of enslaving human life. This Christian woman among others rose to the cause. Millions around the world today are calling out for the same, in desperation for somebody to have a view from the edge of life that is radically different from theirs. People seeing what God sees make a difference in others' lives.

Ralph Waldo Emmerson wrote of the heroes of his day, "But whoso is heroic will always find crises to try his edge." In the times of greatest need–facing a crowd with nothing to eat, or feeling like one lone voice confronting an entire nation against sanctioned slavery, or making a difference where you live and work–those with the edge sharpened by Christ's perspective will cut through.

"God anointed Jesus of Nazareth with the Holy Ghost and with power, who went about doing good and healing all that were oppressed of the devil, for God was with him."[2] Jesus was *confident* even as He walked the edge, because of the anointing of God. He was *compassionate*, using all his Father's resources for "doing good." He was *confrontational*, moving in close to deliver all who were oppressed of the devil, and He was *composed*, no matter how bad or ridiculous or upside down the circumstance, for God was with Him. That's who Jesus was. *And that's who we are if we can see what others miss!*

Most of us don't think we have enough to impact our world. Our circumstances generally speak against that. Most are not wealthy and don't have the "contacts" needed. Most aren't celebrities. I've discovered that most people, beginning with me, are far more aware of what we are not than who God has made us to be.

Pastor Jackson Senyonga was born in Uganda during the reign of Idi Amin, one of the cruelest dictators known to the modern world. He was forsaken to die as a baby. His life was saved, however, and he grew up in an environment full of witchcraft. At fourteen years old, he met his mother for the first time while attending his father's funeral. The following year Jackson gave his life to the Lord and entered ministry training. He was led by the Lord to pioneer a church in the capital city of Uganda, Kampala, with over one million people. Little did he know that this was going to bring a great awakening to his entire city and country. Beginning with seven people, Christian Life Church grew to thousands in weeks and continues to grow by hundreds each week. Within the first year, it had grown to 7000 registered members.

We can be "no way" people. It's easy to be negative, easy to be the one who sits around helping no one.

We can be "I can only do what I can do" people. Seeing only what is immediately at hand, our work will come to an end as soon as our abilities and resources dry up. We'll help a few people in our lifetime, but not much more.

Or, we can choose to be "Father, You can use me to do anything You desire" people. The last time the world saw Someone Who always walked that edge, there was a major revival.

People with a sharpened edge see things from a different view–God's perspective. Seeing things as God sees them, they find possibilities in the midst of impossibilities.

Jesus came to do all that was impossible for man to do alone. "He who sins is of the devil, for the devil has sinned from the beginning. For this purpose the Son of God was manifested, that he might destroy the works of the devil."[3]

God always has a
tomorrow for us that will
require us to
let go of the old if we are
to embrace the new.

"Brethren, I do not count myself to have
apprehended; but one thing I do, forgetting those
things which are behind and reaching
forward to those things which are ahead, I press
toward the goal for the prize of the upward
call of God in Christ Jesus."
Phil 3:13-14

FOUR

UNBLUNTED EDGE

Our edge sharpens almost without effort when we emblazon across our minds, "Citizens of Heaven, Aliens on Earth!" The Apostle Paul said, "For our citizenship is in heaven, from which we also eagerly wait for the Savior, the Lord Jesus Christ." [1] Our ultimate citizenship is not earth, but heaven, from which we also eagerly wait for the Savior, the Lord Jesus Christ.

If we are to live out God's destined purpose for our lives, we cannot afford to be shaped by the values of a world system that the Apostle Paul describes in Scripture. "For many walk, of whom I have told you often, and now tell you even weeping, that they are the enemies of the cross of Christ; whose end is destruction, whose god is their belly, and whose glory is in their shame–who set their mind on earthly things." [2]

One writer noted, "Possession has always blunted the fine edge of altruism." [3]

Some years ago, I remember sitting in my home study surrounded by the effects of eight years of accumulation, none of which was hidden by drawers, desks or tables. My wife Becky was in the middle of redecorating our home. Fresh paint, carpet, wallpaper, countertops, floor tile, and furniture. She had finally convinced me that the living room furniture we'd had for twenty-three years needed replacing.

When she told me it had been over eight years since we'd last redecorated and recovered the furniture, I could hardly believe it. Then I stood on the back of the couch to fix a window covering and heard the fabric rip under my feet–too much harsh Houston sun and too many years. I didn't tell

Becky about the rip, which was hidden in a deep fold in the material. But I did finally concede that maybe it was time for something new.

We moved everything out of closets and cupboards and out from under the beds and to my utter amazement, our possessions alone, without furniture, were enough to fill several rooms–dishes we never ate from, clothes we never wore, assorted gadgets I didn't recognize and couldn't have guessed how to use–some of that stuff I had moved around for twenty years. As Becky's plans took shape, we offered some furniture to young couples in the church, thinking they would pick it up when the new furniture arrived. Instead, they came over immediately and took it, leaving us one chair in the middle of one room and some rooms with no furniture at all.

In the end, how necessary it was to let go of things that had outlived their usefulness, regardless of how comfortable we were with them, in order to embrace the "new" in life. Far more than furniture and household junk are the things we allow to accumulate in our hearts and minds–patterns of thought that seem so comfortable, we don't realize how dull our edges have become.

In all of this I learned a valuable spiritual lesson. In our lives we accumulate the blessings and experiences that are the result of a present season of God's dealings in our lives. But because this life is a journey we are never meant to entrench our lives in a particular season of life regardless of how fruitful it may be. God always has a tomorrow for us that will require us to let go of the old if we are to embrace the new. When God said that His mercies were new every morning, I wonder if He didn't mean that His intent for our lives every day is far grander that we even perceive.

When Becky's plans were finished, I loved the new colors, the new countertops, and the new furniture. I had to clean out the old stuff–wondering why I was keeping all of this junk anyway. One week it seemed immeasurably valuable, the next I couldn't remember why.

We face every new season with either cynicism or faith. Cynicism by its very nature breeds pessimism. Our fears, weariness and dislike of the discomforts involved in change feeds their pessimism. It seems easier to stay just as we are.

What's interesting is that fear is a part of both cynicism and faith. In cynicism, fear deals with you and in faith, you deal with fear.

John Hagee, tells a great story about fear. "Mrs. Monroe lives in Darlington, Maryland. She's the mother of eight children and, except for a few interesting experiences, she's just like any other mother across America. She came home one afternoon from the grocery store and walked into her home. Everything looked pretty much the same, though it was a bit quieter than usual. She looked into the middle of the living room and five of her darlings were sitting around in a circle, exceedingly quiet, doing something in the middle of the circle. She put down the sacks of groceries and walked over closely and saw that they were playing with five of the cutest skunks you can imagine. She was instantly terrified and yelled, "Run, children, run!" Each child grabbed a skunk and ran in five different directions. She was beside herself and screamed louder. It so scared the children that each one squeezed his skunk. And as we all know, skunks don't like to be squeezed."[4]

Maintaining a cutting edge of faith depends on who or what faith is placed in.

I Am
I was regretting the past
And fearing the future ...
Suddenly the Lord was speaking:
"MY NAME IS I AM." He paused.
I waited. He continued.
"WHEN YOU LIVE IN THE PAST,
WITH ITS MISTAKES AND REGRETS,
IT IS HARD, I AM NOT THERE.
MY NAME IS NOT I WAS.
"WHEN YOU LIVE IN THE FUTURE,
WITH ITS PROBLEMS AND FEARS,
IT IS HARD, I AM NOT THERE.
MY NAME IS NOT I WILL BE.
"WHEN YOU LIVE IN THE MOMENT,
IT'S NOT HARD.
I AM HERE.
MY NAME IS I AM."[5]

With faith the size of a mustard seed, mountains will move. Why? Because we don't need a lot of faith when all our faith is placed in a mighty God–a God Who speaks all things into existence and Who calls me to declare, "with God all things are possible[6] ... I am more than a conqueror through Him[7] ... I can do all things through Christ who strengthens me!"[8]

When we know we are citizens of heaven, God's ambassadors to earth, by faith we can embrace each new season anticipating God's faithfulness to us. Like Paul we can say, "forgetting those things which are behind, I press toward the goal for the upward call of God in Christ Jesus."[9]

Every season
passes and we need a
sharp edge to cut
into the next.

"I have been anointed with fresh oil."
Psalm 92:10

FIVE

SHARPENED FOR EVERY SEASON

John F. Kennedy told the nation that we were on the "edge of a new frontier," as America launched into the 1960's. Twenty years later Ronald Reagan said the nation was on the "cutting edge of technology." Perhaps both men were prescient, but probably neither realized how much the nation and the world would really change in the last forty years of the last millennium.

Consider this list compiled for a college faculty to prepare them for the mindset of the young people entering college this year:

1. The people who are starting college this fall are too young to remember the space shuttle blowing up.
2. Their lifetime has always included AIDS.
3. The CD was introduced the year they were born.
4. They have always had an answering machine and cable TV.
5. Jay Leno has always been on the Tonight Show.
6. Popcorn has always been cooked in the microwave.
7. They never took a swim and thought about Jaws.
8. They can't imagine what hard contact lenses are.
9. They don't know who Mork was or where he was from.
10. They've never heard:
    a. "Where's the Beef?"
    b. "I'd walk a mile for a Camel"
    c. "de plane Boss, de plane"
11. They do not care who shot J. R. and have no idea who J. R. even is.

12. McDonald's never came in Styrofoam containers.

13. They don't have a clue how to use a typewriter.[1]

Each of us enter new seasons and situations surrounded by the accumulation of the years we have lived; knowledge we've acquired; ideas developed or left idle; plans completed or never started; tragedies suffered; triumphs enjoyed. Every season passes, and we need a sharp edge to cut into the next.

We often look at youth and admire the carefree attitude, the willingness to risk, and as the years pile up, perhaps we forget that we too have choices. We can continue to live weighted down with the stuff of past years, or we can look beyond what we have grown comfortable with and embrace new ideas and new possibilities.

We enter Christ's kingdom in a wave of glory, start avenues of ministry with conviction, launch businesses and careers with determination, yet it is amazing to look back and see how dull our edges have become. How does it happen?

My entire family took a vacation one year, the events of which provided a great object lesson for me in my own ministry. We went to one of the white sand beaches in Florida with our two daughters, their husbands and our four grandchildren. Out of convenience, and at the request of the grandchildren, the entire family went to Taco Bell one evening to pick up a quick dinner. Having opted for "better" Mexican food found in "real" restaurants, I hadn't been to a Taco Bell in years. While waiting for our order, I noticed a sign–"All Food Made Fresh While You Wait." I'm not sure if it really tasted fresher, or if it was because of the sign, but it seemed to be better food than I'd remembered back in my fast food days. It made me think about the meaning of "fresh."

We live in a world desperately in need of "fresh" ministry. Outside of national crises that brings religion to the fore, our culture has largely written off the Church. Terms like "not relevant" are used to describe our condition. It seems to me that relevancy is what flows out of freshness. Relevancy isn't about style (how you do what you are called to do), but about fresh anointing.

Staying fresh–it's the constant challenge every Christian faces. Pursuing a career, raising a family, caring for aging parents, engaging at least in occasional recreation, making purchases, investments, future planning ... all these can squeeze us off the edge. We can be consumed by the hectic pace of the day in which we live and the demands of our schedules–confronted by the subtle and not so subtle attacks of hell that stifle our creativity and endeavor to lower our opinion of our value to the Lord–exposed to the wounding of people who out of their own turmoil and brokenness many times attack us personally–discouraged by the lack of apparent visible results in our lives, especially when compared with others (there is always someone who's having more results than you)–depleted by violating the basic disciplines of personal growth that allow faith to rule instead of doubt. These conditions left without treatment become overwhelming. They sap our strength and produce weariness and stagnation.

When we are fresh, sharp, honed to cut through, the areas of conflict and adversity we all face are easily overcome because we know the battle is the Lord's. "They overcame him by the blood of the lamb and the word of their testimony."[2] We meet Hell's tactics, life's mountains, and ministry challenges with a piercing declaration of God's ability and His faithfulness to us in every situation. We recognize that we are overcomers by the blood of the Lamb. Our testimony is like a sharpened sword–quick and powerful.

When we are not fresh, and dulled in our spirits and minds, the same things become overwhelming–larger than us–and though we know they are not larger than God, we can't seem to find the keys to release His provision. We find ourselves plunging deeper into the abyss of confusion and despair, resulting in that "existence" mindset that still believes God is God, but doesn't have the assurance that He will fulfill our destiny, or use us as we once thought He would. We go through the motions with something missing. When we're honest with ourselves, we admit that the God-breathed Holy Spirit-anointed spark that gives life to our talents and giftings is gone.

It is amazing how long we can run on empty by relying on our natural abilities. Even pastors can rely on the "machines" we've built. But sooner or later, without the oil of the Spirit of God in our machine, we break down and lose the distinction of having God-breathed supernatural power added to our own abilities. When that happens, we begin to smell like "flesh" and the odor of flesh turns off a world desperately searching for reality.

How do we get there? How do our edges become so blunted that we can't cut through the smallest problem?

On that family vacation, my four-year-old granddaughter Madison thoroughly enjoyed the water's edge. She came in from the beach late one afternoon, and my daughter decided to clean her up enough for dinner, then bathe her later. But as she attempted to comb Madison's thick hair, she could hardly move the brush. You couldn't see it, but Madison's hair had filled with sand. She hadn't dumped a bucket of sand on her head while playing. Just the wind blowing the sand, one grain at a time, built up in her hair to the point that it required several washings to get out.

In the same way, we lose our freshness from a buildup over time, not overnight. We become stale and lifeless in our spirits one grain at a time. The wind blows in one situation at a time, one challenge at a time that requires the life flow of the Holy Spirit to energize us. Soon we don't notice that the demand for effective ministry is drawing down our reservoir of His presence within us. Unless His Spirit presence and power is replenished, we soon stand on empty, with no reserves. With that emptiness comes the tendency for isolation and loneliness, compounding the problems we already have.

How can we stay fresh? As one who knows the exhilarating joy of freshness and also the devastating agony of depletion, I can attest to the fact that no one-time shots can fix "fresh" forever. *Staying fresh, sharp, focused is a daily thing.*

God's mercies are "new every morning."[3] Your greatest challenge in living a vibrant Christian life will always be an every-morning freshness, where each day you rediscover the great faithfulness of God.

You cannot sharpen yourself without ongoing encounters with a life-giving God. You must come to know the God of the Word. The approach can vary depending upon our personality and lifestyle. You have to find out what works best for you. It has to become a discipline that when ignored compels you to get back quickly.

This is the most important component by far in staying fresh–yet there are others. I've discovered that books, tapes and seminars help keep my risk factor low, my faith high, and my challenges in perspective. Rest and relaxation allow me to recuperate from exhausting demands and help my creativity to flow. Physical exercise keeps up my energy level and helps equip me to run life's race with endurance. Key relationships help keep me on track and provide the support I need to finish well.

All of these are ongoing things, most done on a consistent basis. All require quality time. My biggest regret in life is that I didn't learn sooner how to sharpen these edges.

Life is a journey, a race, a course. One season helps prepare us for the next. We must never grow comfortable with stale pasts as we press into new futures.

"Not that I have already attained or am already perfected; but I press on, that I may lay hold of that for which Christ Jesus has also laid hold of me."[4]

The key to "pressing on" is found in that simple sign I saw in that Taco Bell–"made fresh while you wait."

I can never
forget that I am called
to serve.

"Whoever desires to become great among
you, let him be your servant."
Matthew 20:26

TUGGED TO THE EDGE

Sharpened spiritually and ready to hear the voice of the Lord, you will find that God tugs you to the edge, to a place of divine purpose, with a gentle calling to your spirit. One day recently, I felt the Lord's tug on my heart several times during the day. The Holy Spirit was dealing with me to telephone a friend of mine who was going through a very trying time.

Around eight o'clock that night–after a day of numerous meetings, appointments and phone calls, some of which were especially draining and exhausting–I was ready to head home and crash. Three attempts to contact my friend had proved fruitless. As I prepared to leave my office, I knew I should try again, but my flesh argued against another attempt. I was weary, and I'd already tried to respond to the Lord's request. Wasn't that enough?

I had already turned off the lights of the office when I went back, sat down and dialed the number again. That call led to another appointment for the day, a Spirit-ordained meeting. When my friend answered, I opened the conversation by relating how the Lord had dealt with me throughout the day. His response conveyed an obvious, urgent need for this moment. That call opened the door where the Lord allowed me the privilege of imparting His life in a desperate situation. As I drove home two hours later, I marveled at how right the timing of the Lord was.

In the "busyness" of life–for me, the programs and business of ministry–a sharp focus allows us to be led to the edge where God needs one of Heaven's citizens in compassion and mercy to take authority in a situation in the earth.

Through these times, the Lord refreshes and renews His priorities in us.

As I keep myself daily fresh, invigorated by God's Spirit, my heart must break over the things that break the Lord's. Mankind going its own way with a destructive vengeance must cause a wrenching of my spirit. Compassion and weeping must well up within me for the people around me, and those the Lord has entrusted to me. Their problems and struggles must touch me, and when they do, I must pray with a tenacity that invades the impossible.

Alan Redpath writes: "You never lighten the load unless first you have felt the pressure in your own soul. You are never used of God to bring blessing until God has opened your eyes and made you see things as they are."[1] Nehemiah was called to build the wall, but first he wept over ruins.

We need to allow our hearts to break. This story was sent to me via email from an anonymous source:

She was six years old when I first met her on the beach near where I live. I drive to this beach, a distance of three or four miles, whenever the world begins to close in on me. She was building a sandcastle or something and looked up, her eyes as blue as the sea.

"Hello," she said.

I answered with a nod, not really in the mood to bother with a small child.

"I'm building," she said.

"I see that. What is it?" I asked, not caring.

"Oh, I don't know, I just like the feel of the sand."

That sounds good, I thought, and slipped off my shoes. A sandpiper glided by.

"That's a joy," the child said.

"It's a what?"

"It's a joy. My mama says sandpipers come to bring us joy." The bird went gliding down the beach.

"Good-bye job," I muttered to myself, "hello pain," and turned to walk on. I was depressed. My life seemed completely out of balance.

"What's your name?" She wouldn't give up.

"Robert," I answered. "I'm Robert Peterson."

"Mine's Wendy ... I'm six."

"Hi Wendy."

She giggled. "You're funny," she said.

In spite of my gloom I laughed too and walked on. Her musical giggle followed me.

"Come again Mr. P," she called. "We'll have another happy day."

The days and weeks that followed belonged to others: a group of unruly Boy Scouts, PTA meetings, and an ailing mother. The sun was shining one morning as I took my hands out of the dishwater.

"I need a sandpiper," I said to myself, gathering up my coat. The ever-changing balm of the seashore awaited me. The breeze was chilly, but I strode along trying to recapture the serenity I needed. I had forgotten the child and was startled when she appeared.

"Hello, Mr. P," she said. "Do you want to play?"

"What did you have in mind?" I asked, with a twinge of annoyance.

"I don't know. You say."

"How about charades?" I asked sarcastically.

The tinkling laughter burst forth again. "I don't know what that is."

"Then let's just walk." Looking at her, I noticed the delicate fairness of her face. "Where do you live?" I asked.

"Over there." She pointed toward a row of summer cottages. Strange, I thought, in winter.

"Where do you go to school?"

"I don't go to school. Mommy says we're on vacation." She chattered little girl talk as we strolled up the beach, but my mind was on other things. When I left for home, Wendy said it had been a happy day. Feeling surprisingly better, I smiled at her and agreed.

Three weeks later, I rushed to my beach in a state of near panic. I was in no mood even to greet Wendy. I thought I saw her mother on the porch and felt like demanding she keep her child at home.

"Look, if you don't mind," I said crossly when Wendy caught up with me, I'd rather be alone today."

She seemed unusually pale and out of breath. "Why?" she asked.

I turned to her and shouted, "Because my mother died!" I thought, why was I saying this to a little child?

"Oh," she said quietly, "then this is a sad day."

"Yes," I said, "and yesterday and the day before and–oh, go away!"

"Did it hurt?" she inquired.

"Did what hurt?" I was exasperated with her–with myself.

"When she died?"

"Of course it hurt!" I snapped, misunderstanding. Wrapped up in myself. I strode off.

A month or so after that, when I next went to the beach, she wasn't there. Feeling guilty, ashamed and admitting to myself I missed her, I went up to the cottage after my walk and knocked on the door. A drawn-looking young woman with honey-colored hair opened the door.

"Hello," I said, "I'm Robert Peterson. I missed your little girl today and wondered where she was."

"Oh yes, Mr. Peterson, please come in. Wendy spoke of you so much. I'm afraid I allowed her to bother you. If she was a nuisance, please, accept my apologies."

"Not at all–she is a delightful child," I said, suddenly realizing that I meant what I had just said.

"Wendy died last week, Mr. Peterson. She had leukemia. Maybe she didn't tell you."

Struck dumb, I groped for a chair. I had to catch my breath.

"She loved this beach, so when she asked to come, we couldn't say no. She seemed so much better here and had a lot of what she called happy days. But the last few weeks, she declined rapidly ..." Her voice faltering, she said, "She left something for you ... if only I can find it. Could you wait a moment while I look?"

I nodded stupidly, my mind racing for something to say to this lovely young woman. She handed me a smeared envelope with Mr. P printed in childish letters. Inside was a drawing in bright crayon of a yellow beach, a blue sea, and a brown bird. Underneath was carefully printed: A SANDPIPER TO BRING YOU JOY. Tears welled up in my eyes and a heart that had almost forgotten to love opened wide. I took Wendy's mother in my arms. "I'm so sorry, I'm so sorry, I'm so sorry," I muttered over and over again, and we wept together.

The precious little picture is framed now and hangs in my study. Six words–one for each year of her life–that speak to me of harmony, courage, and undemanding love. A gift from a child with sea-blue eyes and hair the color of sand–who taught me the gift of love.

I can never forget that I am called to serve, not to be served. The "pedestal mentality" of modern Christianity many times directs more glory to the man than to the Lord. It is easy to become mechanical, directing an organization and receiving acclaim. The foundation of all fulfillment in life has to do with giving our lives away.

Giving and serving is what each of us is called to do. We must be continually filled if we expect to continually give. People don't need us as desperately as they need Jesus in us. I like how a Baptist pastor in our city prays before he speaks: "Let me get out of the way that people might see You."

As I write these words I can hear the voice of my friend Doug Stringer ringing with conviction and passion filling my soul– "While men reach for thrones to build their own kingdoms, Jesus reached for a towel to wash men's feet."

Unless we have
the edge of His presence–
we have no life.

"In Him we live and move and have our being."
Acts 17:28

SEVEN

CUTTING-EDGE PRESENCE

The call of God is always upward. My response to His call is to keep pressing toward God's purpose in me. "Brethren, I do not count myself to have apprehended; but one thing I do, forgetting those things which are behind and reaching forward to those things which are ahead, I press toward the goal for the prize of the upward call of God in Christ Jesus."[1]

Revival, renewal, refreshing ... all are terms used to describe a fresh entry of the Lord into the human scene. We know we want a fresh entry from Him, yet it always amazes me how quickly we reject anything that doesn't carry the label or form with which we are comfortable. We get so hung up believing that if everyone loved God as much as we do, they would naturally do things our way. Many times we become only spectators and "fruit inspectors" of valid moves of God—explaining why God can't do something a certain way, or move on certain people because what He does violates our comfort zone.

We pray for revival, then reject the form it comes in—seems ridiculous, doesn't it? In the same way, a previous generation of godly men and women called out to God for a Saviour, then rejected the Messiah. It's been written, "Human beings, who are almost unique in having the ability to learn from the experience of others, are also remarkable for their apparent disinclination to do so."[2] We get hung up on terms or methods, even though we know previous generations that got hung up on terms or methods failed to realize the day of their salvation.

Most of us come to the Lord as a result of a special out-pouring. As our move of God runs its course, we can't understand why God would do things differently. We then begin to make the *methodology* of our season of refreshing holy. Certain outward behavior becomes synonymous with holiness, rather than holiness being an issue of our heart that manifests itself in Godly living.

Certain actions and terms become synonymous with God's presence, whether there is any life left in them or not. We become spiritually arrogant–rejecting all other experiences of the grace of God as shallow, heresy, or even "of the devil." We somehow ignore or explain away the excesses and errors of when God moved "our way" but can't tolerate excess or error when He moves differently than He did with us.

All the time we are building a spiritual museum that enshrines the best of our revival. We polish and perfect our methods and don't even realize that the "life" (Holy Spirit presence) is slowly waning. "Museum?" Maybe I should say "tomb." We ultimately become Pharisees. Our acceptance of others now requires adherence to legalistic behavior that only affects the outward man but doesn't transform his inward attitudes. For example, we condemn the act of physical adultery, but participate in sexual fantasy. We condemn outward vices like drinking and smoking but allow lying, bitterness, gossip, envy, and sowing discord among brethren. It comes into our lives and into those around us, but we explain this behavior away as, "That's just how I am (or how they are)." Yet those are the very things God says He hates.

When we've lost the edge of God's presence, we have also lost true conviction. Our convictions become established by our own set of values instead of God's Word. Those convictions are at best inconsistent, and at worst points of bondage. Jesus said it best when talking about the Pharisees–we become like whitewashed tombs full of dead men's bones.[3] The outside, our best methods from our renewal in God, is well preserved. We still do everything we did when God was around all the time. But inside we're dead. We're dead because unless we have the edge of His presence, we have no life.

A number of years ago, out of a fresh encounter with the Lord that radically changed both of our lives, Becky wrote the following:

I'm not sure if I can articulate accurately what God has done in me, but all I know is He has done a very deep inner work that continues to happen. It's as if He said, "Becky, look at me."

Have you ever talked with someone who while you are talking their eyes are wandering, looking about, not really paying attention to you? What you really want to do is take their face in your hands and say, "Look at me! I want your full attention. I'm trying to tell you something."

Well, that's what I feel God has done to me. He took His hands and gently placed them on my face and said, "Becky, look at me. Don't be distracted by everything else around you. Don't be so busy working for Me, caught up in the work, that you don't see Me, because everything you will ever need, everything that is fulfillment is in me. I want your full attention. Look at me. See me in all my glory, power and might."

I then saw hundreds of beautifully wrapped boxes with beautiful bows and people were sitting on top of these boxes. What I realized is we had put God in a box. Oh, it was a beautiful box. Anyone looking upon it would say what a beautiful wrapping and bow, but what was really happening is that we had said to God, "You stay right here within these boundaries. I'll let You move right here. Don't do anything that is out of my comfort zone. Don't demand too much time. I have things to do, schedules to keep. If You move outside of here it might scare me and what will others think. This is a nice, respectable way to serve You."

Then God said to me, "Becky, you've put me in a box."

I was shocked. I said, "Oh, no, God, I haven't done that."

He said, "Yes, you have."

I wept. I asked for forgiveness. I didn't realize I had done that. I've always had a heart for God, but He exposed something I didn't see. I repented and I've taken the lid off the box of limitation. I've declared that in my life–God, you be God. I don't care what you do to me, through me, and around me–You Be God!!

Pentecostal Revival, Charismatic Renewal, Third Wave, Refreshing, Blessing, Outpouring–I have no interest in terms. I am absolutely committed to being a part of what God is doing in the earth in this day and staying on the edge of His presence. That alone will keep me from a pharisaic rigidity that would allow the methods of this day or any other to cause me to miss out on a present outpouring of God's Spirit.

In the Old Testament, great value was placed on the establishment of spiritual monuments. They were never meant to be worshipped, but were to be points of remembrance of the past faithfulness of God to a present generation who walk by faith in their present discovery of this awesome God.

Worship is first about what I am, and then it is about what I do.

"He has shown you, O Man,
what is good and what does the Lord require of
you? But to do justly, to love mercy,
and to walk humbly with your God."
Micah 6:8

EIGHT

THE HEART'S EDGE

Children were asked how to tell in a restaurant if someone is in love. One little girl answered, "It's love if they order one of those desserts that are on fire. They like to order those because it's just like how their hearts are–on fire."

Lovers' hearts burn inside them. That kind of love toward God–a love that consumes us–comes from a heart on the edge. But how do you keep your heart fires burning? Your family's? Your church's? How do you navigate the minefields of hell that threaten to destroy any possibility for you, your ministry or your church being a force for the Kingdom of God for the long haul? How do you stay effective?

Yes, we must learn to live on the edge, recognizing God's timing and perspective, freeing ourselves from distracting clutter, sharpening our hearts to listen and obey, and accepting new ways in which God manifests His presence. But what can we do to ensure we are in position to fulfill God's call on our lives?

Two broad areas of the heart need ongoing attention. First is personal discipline–our private, personal walk with God. The second is relationship.

The first is centered in worship. Worship is the heart's edge, the ultimate purpose of our creation. Out of worship flows God's creativity, revelation, direction, ministry. But, worship is one of those areas in which we have a tendency to believe that *our* approach is the *right* approach. Again, that mindset dulls our edge and, besides having a smell of spiritual arrogance, it is totally rooted in taste. In worship, the concerns tend to center around music style, volume, atmosphere, and physical manifestations rather than the substance of a heart that cries out to God regardless of how it happens to be done.

Over the years, I have had a keen interest in worship. *What is true worship?* Many years ago I was standing in a worship service hundreds of miles from where we lived. The auditorium was filled with hundreds of people. There was an obvious sense of God's presence in the room. The congregation was singing one of the old hymns of the church that spoke of the majesty and glory of God. We had long since put our hymnals aside and sung only the latest contemporary music. Without realizing it, a smugness that we were more "with it" had encrusted my soul and God was about to confront my attitude of being spiritually superior.

I remember thinking, "If these people knew what we know and worshipped like we do, they would really have something here." I no sooner thought those words than I heard this voice, "What's the matter? You can't worship Me in a hymn?"

I realized later that it wasn't audible, but it might as well have been. It so startled me that I opened my eyes to look around to see who was talking to me. Everyone around me had their eyes closed in worship. It was then I realized that God had challenged my arrogance. It was like a knife to my heart. My instant response was– "Yes Lord, I can worship you in a hymn, with music, or without music."

To this day, that encounter with the Lord profoundly impacts me and challenges me to passionately pursue vital, fresh, heart's-edge worship of the One who is far larger than any particular style.

How do you worship the Lord? *What happens when you do?*

Out of my personal journey to walk not only in God's way, but also to know Him intimately and to be a true worshipper, I have made a few observations. I discovered that worship is not first about what I do. Worship is first about what I *am*, then it is about what I *do*.

I can *do* worship without *being* a worshipper. This is one of the pitfalls for Christians, particularly those in leadership ministry. The demands of a ministry calling may be so consuming–the pressure of public image so important–that we succumb to a place where we become good at going through the motions and emotions of worship without truly worshipping.

My heart and my flesh crying out for the living God continually confront issues in my life that challenge me to walk with an inward integrity and outward obedience to His way. "He has shown you, O man, what is good; and what does the Lord require of you But to do justly, to love mercy, and to walk humbly with your God."[1]

For me, though I greatly enjoy the emotional aspect of worship, a far better integrity check on how I am doing as a worshipper is in answering the following hard questions:

Am I:
- consistently in awe of the God I serve?
- dependent instead of independent?
- honest and truthful?
- pliable and changeable?
- genuinely humble?
- challenged to live beyond myself?

These are heart-edge questions, to be answered with integrity only by examining your heart and inviting the Holy Spirit to do the same. The other examination of the heart's edge comes in relationships, and specifically in relationships that fulfill the Biblical mandate of promoting unity among believers. The Bible says:

"Behold, how good and how pleasant it is for brethren to dwell together in unity."[2]

"By this all will know that you are My disciples, if you have love for one another."[3]

During decades as a senior pastor, I have been involved with numerous efforts to unify the Church. I've discovered that organized efforts to unify the Church have only limited success and generally don't last long. I think it's because efforts to unify the Church can only succeed if the leadership has an attitude of unity. If all we are saying is, "Let's unite, so long as I'm in charge," then we will never see true unity. True unity in the Church of Jesus begins with *me*.

How can we promote unity? What are the things I need to pay attention to and what do I need to avoid? Here are two ways that are short when written, but can take a lifetime of discipline to achieve:

> 1. *Treat others as you want to be treated.* Be genuinely humble and accepting of others and let God exalt you instead of being manipulative. Keep reminding yourself that if someone loves Jesus, we are all on the same side. Fight against the rise of a competitive spirit within you. Never, never, never be condescending. Recognize the tendency to spiritual superiority that is in each of us. Make your circle of acceptance as wide as Jesus would.
>
> I was raised by parents who loved God and I was in one denomination through my early twenties. It was never said, but I grew up believing that if everyone

else really saw the light they would be a part of our denomination. After all, we had the whole truth. It wasn't anything I spent time thinking about, but it was something that colored my view of how I saw "other" Christians who were not a part of us.

When Becky and I set out to begin our ministry as senior pastors we felt led of the Lord to plant a church in a city in Northern California. The problem was that the pastor of the one church of our denomination in that city didn't want us there and we had to surrender our credentials if we were to do what we felt God was telling us to do. I can still remember the feeling of "lostness" and despair because we thought we had given up a promising future for what seemed to be an insurmountable challenge. What was really happening was that God was opening up to us a big new world that we would never have seen or embraced had He not taken us this way. Along the way we learned to appreciate the rich diversity of the Body of Christ. We discovered that God's circle of acceptance looked a whole lot different than ours and was a whole lot larger.

2. *Make sure the Cross is the qualifying factor.* Worship styles, methodology, opinions, and doctrinal differences that are more man's idea than God's Word should never divide. Appreciate the diversity within the Body of Christ and recognize that those who think differently than you can still love Jesus as much as you do. Keep asking yourself what

would Jesus do, say, and so on. Or even, what DID Jesus do, say, and so on? Practice giving yourself away as Jesus asked.

Here is another heart-check. To stand in integrity, examine your own heart and ask the Holy Spirit to do the same:

- Is my first evaluation of someone else negative–looking for what's wrong, sizing them up? *(If so, you need to change!)*
- Is my practice only to be a part of things that benefit me or what I am doing?
- Do I tend to isolate myself? *(You can't be isolated and unified at the same time.)*
- Can I identify with brothers and sisters in leadership–"rejoice with those who rejoice and weep with those who weep"?[4]
- Am I prone always to build up–or to tear down?
- Will I allow gossip, strife, envy, jealousy, and such to come into me and pass on to others? *(These kill any hope of unity.)*

Unity is a choice. You are either contributing to unity, or you're taking away from the possibility of it ever happening in Jesus' Church. It's a matter of sharpening your heart's edge.

There is no substitute
for the strength you receive
from authentic
relationships.

"Consider one another in order to stir up
love and good works."
Hebrews 10:24

NINE

THE LEADER'S EDGE

Hours behind the runner in front of him, the last marathoner finally entered the Olympic stadium. By that time, the drama of the day's events was almost over and most of the spectators had gone home. This athlete's story, however, was still being played out. Limping into the arena, the Tanzanian runner grimaced with every step, his knee bleeding and bandaged from an earlier fall. His ragged appearance immediately caught the attention of the remaining crowd, who cheered him on to the finish line. Why did he stay in the race? What made him endure his injuries to the end? When asked these questions later, he replied, "My country did not send me 7,000 miles away to start the race. They sent me 7,000 miles to finish it."[1]

The question is–How do we do that? What are the things we should give priority to that strengthen and energize us for the journey? The most important one I know after taking care of your private walk with God is walking together with other leaders in community.

There is no substitute for the strength you receive from authentic relationships. Everything in our fast-paced world argues against our investment in true community. As leaders, we tend to know more about pastors "in the community" than we do about pastors "in community." I am extremely grateful for the ministry peers who are an integral part of my life. I highly value the men who will speak honestly to me, who encourage me, who I can say anything to and know I will be accepted, embraced, and given wise counsel. I've discovered that "God's way" for me contains a lot of challenges I would not necessarily embrace on my own. I need those who walk where I walk to help me sort it out.

God's future and hope for me stretches me to the max and without the encouragement of true friends I'm convinced I'd never go for all that God has for me. My friend of more than twenty-five years is Paul Adams. I am thinking of all the times he has "been there" for me.

Twenty-four years ago Paul ran around a van with bullets flying everywhere, pulled me out and laid me on the ground. I lay there with seven stab wounds inflicted by prisoners in a Philippine prison where we had been ministering. Paul got me to a hospital and cared for me until I could fly home. He then flew halfway around the world with me to make sure I made it.

When God led me to leave my pastorate of ten years and move on to Houston, Texas, where I had never been, to start all over with nothing, Paul was there with counsel and support. He helped pay my bills those first few months.

When my children were married, he was there. When my youngest daughter and her husband wanted to adopt a baby, he found that precious little girl. When I walked through my deepest crisis moments, both personal and in ministry, he was a wise confidant and encourager. We have loaned each other money–my house is his house. Whatever he needs, if I can, it's his and the same goes the other way.

And more than that God has given me other men who walk with me that same way. My life has been enriched because of them. I'm convinced I would be a statistic today, a casualty of ministry, disillusioned and emotionally broken without the nurture and support of these men in community.

The challenges of our day are revealing both the best and

the worst of the leadership community. The divorce rate among leaders is alarming. Pornography is an insidious destroyer. We are no longer shocked when a pastor falls morally. Discouragement and defeat cause record numbers to leave vocational ministry. The everyday grind of pressure and stress takes its toll on us and threatens to drain our ability to take the heat.

At the same time, the cry for a move of God by a praying Church is unlike anything I've seen in my lifetime. In city after city, pastors and churches are joining together to worship and relate to one another as members of Christ's Body. Polls tell us that the American society is "spiritually minded," even if it is other spirits. That tells us people are searching for reality. As those who lead, we must be spiritually, mentally, and physically on edge–energized and ready.

If you are a leader or pastor, who are the ministry peers with whom you share your heart? To whom can you tell your deepest secrets? Who can you share your temptations with that will stand with you in prayer and counsel? Who can you ask for help with the struggles of being a minister of God? Where do you go with the struggles that stem from being formed into a pastor of power and also a person in the process?

All of these questions can be answered by pastoral community–the necessity of deepening relationships with those of similar calling. I have discovered that the challenge of impacting a city of five million takes on a whole new anticipation of fruitfulness when shared in community with those "called" as I am. Authentic truth-telling, sharing, intimacy, shared strength, support, faith, and fresh focus are benefits of being in community with other pastors.

"Lone rangers" set themselves up for failure. Community begins with intentional acts, started by developing friendships. This is a day that calls for all of us to link our arms with one another, supporting and uplifting one another, and to bless each other toward His fruitfulness through our differing assignments.

excellent

What is unity? Unity: (1) the state of being one; (2) the quality of being one in spirit; (3) an arrangement of parts or material that will produce a single harmonious design; (4) a union of related parts.[2]

Probably no other word is so easy to define, and difficult to live out as this one. Much of the time, man's interpretation and God's are quite different. Anyone who reads the scripture with objectivity discovers that God speaks of unity in terms of a common foundation, but with great diversity regarding individual points of style, preference and personality.

In God's divine wisdom, He calls for all of these individual parts to flow together in a common cause (Jesus Christ) and appreciation for each others' giftings and placement in Christ's Body. "But now God has set the members, each one of them, in the body just as He pleased. And if they were all one member, where would the body be? But now indeed there are many members, yet one body."[3]

Dwelling together in unity requires some practical decisions that begin with acknowledging that God created diversity when He made people uniquely different, yet basically the same. Diversity isn't the invention of man, nor the work of the devil–it is God's plan. In other words, people's preference in worship and church style is natural.

We must move beyond the externals and come to recognize "heart" in people. By that, I mean someone who has a different "spiritual taste" than you, can love God every bit as much as you do and have a heart edge every bit as yours. After all, we are not spiritual clones of a certain ecclesiastical system. We are people on the way–becoming–being conformed to Christ, which is first an inward work in our hearts before outward manifestation is ever seen.[4]

Phariseeism, on the other hand, has to do with those who consider the outside more important than the inside. Whenever we succumb to Phariseeism, we become spiritually arrogant and find ourselves manifesting those actions God said He hated: "These six things the Lord hates, Yes, seven are an abomination to Him: A proud look, a lying tongue, hands that shed innocent blood, A heart that devises wicked plans, feet that are swift in running to evil, a false witness who speaks lies, and one who sows discord among brethren."[5]

It seems wise to stay far away from anything God so objects to that He says He hates it. None of us like slander, gossip, lies or trouble stirred up because we all know the devastation it causes. Those attitudes and actions in congregations destroy churches and stymie Kingdom advancement. God's program stops while we try to get people to get along.

Unfortunately, many times we indulge in the very things we are opposed to. We are all good at rationalizing our behavior, so we may let things like strife and backbiting slide even though we find them reprehensible in others. But if it continues, it will no longer be limited to a season of unrest, but will become a permanent part of our demeanor as we become cynical toward everything.

"Cynical" sounds a bit gentle compared to Scripture. James wrote about it this way: "But no man can tame the tongue. It is an unruly evil, full of deadly poison. With it we bless our God and Father, and with it we curse men, who have been made in the similitude of God. Out of the same mouth proceed blessing and cursing. My brethren, these things ought not to be so. Does a spring send forth fresh water and bitter from the same opening? Can a fig tree, my brethren, bear olives, or a grapevine bear figs? Thus no spring yields both salt water and fresh."[6] James 3:8-12

We lose our edge, becoming unproductive in God's Kingdom, never living up to our potential, when we gossip or engage in slander and judge instead of pursuing unity. Rather than being a blessing, we actually become a curse–even dragging others into the same abyss.

Unity is important because it is the requirement for Christ's body to function.[7] Without an appreciation for everyone in Christ's body and with the full acknowledgement that He is the One who places each one of us, we become weak and sickly, and some even die because we fail to discern His body.[8]

How desperately we need each other! Take a fresh look at a familiar passage: "I, therefore, the prisoner of the Lord, beseech you to walk worthy of the calling with which you were called, with all lowliness and gentleness, with longsuffering, bearing with one another in love, endeavoring to keep the unity of the Spirit in the bond of peace. There is one body and one Spirit, just as you were called in one hope of your calling; one Lord, one faith, one baptism; one God and Father of all, who is above all, and through all, and in you all. But to each one of us grace was given according to the measure of Christ's gift."[9] Eph 4:1-7

Without spiritual passion, your gifting and talent won't matter.

"Stir up the gift of God which is in you."
II Timothy 1:6

TEN

PASSIONATE EDGE

"That's edgy." I hear the younger generation use this phrase to describe something that's almost too much. It's beyond normal, regular, pressing the boundaries. That's how we're called to live.

David Berman said it well. "Suppose someone gave you a pen–a sealed, solid-colored pen. You couldn't see how much ink it had. It might run dry after the first few tentative words or last just long enough to create a masterpiece (or several) that would last forever and make a difference in the scheme of things. You don't know before you begin. Under the rules of the game, you really never know. You have to take a chance!

"Actually, no rules of the game state you must do anything. Instead of picking up and using the pen, you could leave it on a shelf or in a drawer where it will dry up, unused. But if you decide to use it, what would you do with it? How would you play the game? Would you plan and plan before you ever wrote a word? Would your plans be so extensive that you never even get to the writing? Or would you take the pen in hand, plunge right in and just do it, struggling to keep up with the twists and turns of the torrents of words that take you where they take you?

"Would you write cautiously and carefully, as if the pen might run dry the next moment, or would you pretend or believe (or pretend to believe) that the pen will write forever and proceed accordingly? And of what would you write: Of love? Hate? Fun? Misery? Life? Death? Nothing? Everything? Would you write to please just yourself? Or others? Or yourself by writing for others? Would your strokes be tremblingly timid or brilliantly bold? Fancy with a flourish or plain? Would you even write?

"Once you have the pen, no rule says you have to write. Would you sketch? Scribble? Doodle or draw? Would you stay in or on the lines, or see no lines at all, even if they were there? Or are they? There's a lot to think about here, isn't there? Now, suppose someone gave you a life ..."[1]

Life must have purpose. No one likes to be labeled "immature." Not in our attitudes, work habits, certainly not when arguing with a spouse. But what is maturity? *True Biblical maturity can be defined as understanding and living a purpose-driven life.*

"Therefore let us, as many as are mature, have this mind; and if in anything you think otherwise, God will reveal even this to you."[2]

What is your purpose? And are you driven toward it with passion? Without spiritual passion, your gifting and talent won't matter. The Apostle Paul exhorted his son in the Lord, Timothy to "... stir up the gift of God which is in you ..."[3] He wanted Timothy to keep a passionate edge–to stay excited, on fire, stirred up inside. Other translations of this passage are equally emphatic:

Message Bible:	"The special gift of ministry you received–keep it ablaze."
New Living Bible:	"Fan into flames the spiritual gift God gave you."
Amplified:	"Stir up, (rekindle the embers of, fan the flame of, and keep burning) the (gracious) gift of God."

Spiritual passion requires first a calling from God that ignites a fire within us–then our continued stoking of the fire that we might be passionate in ministering with our gifting.

I've wondered many times what happened to people who had an obvious call of God on their lives, but seemed to settle for just getting by. The call to ministry by the Lord over time became a job–the means to pay the rent, the bills, buy food, and so forth.

After decades of being a senior pastor, I've been through enough challenges, faced enough obstacles, walked through enough discouraging times to know that there's plenty of stuff we all find in life to douse the flames of spiritual passion. So I'm very much intrigued by Paul saying to Timothy: *You* stir it up! *You* fan the flames. It seems to me that stirring and fanning are things God ought to do. But, if indeed the fanning part is up to me–what does that mean in a practical sense?

I can sum it up in two words–choices and commitments. These will keep up your passion.

The little country schoolhouse was heated by an old-fashioned, potbellied coal stove. A little boy had the job of coming to school early each day to start the fire and warm the room before his teacher and his classmates arrived.

One morning they arrived to find the schoolhouse engulfed in flames. They dragged the unconscious little boy out of the flaming building more dead than alive. He had major burns over the lower half of his body and was taken to the nearby county hospital.

From his bed the dreadfully burned, semi-conscious little boy faintly heard the doctor talking to his mother. The doctor told his mother that her son would surely die–which was for the best, really–for the terrible fire had devastated the lower half of his body. But the brave boy didn't want to die. He made up his mind that he would survive. Somehow, to the amazement of the physician, he did survive.

When the mortal danger was past, he again heard the doctor and his mother speaking quietly. The mother was told that since the fire had destroyed so much flesh in the lower part of his body, it would almost be better if he had died, since he was doomed to be a lifetime cripple with no use at all of his lower limbs. Once more the brave boy made up his mind. He would not be a cripple. He would walk. But unfortunately from the waist down, he had no motor ability. His thin legs just dangled there, all but lifeless.

Ultimately the boy was released from the hospital. Every day his mother would massage his little legs, but there was no feeling, no control, nothing. Yet his determination that he would walk was as strong as ever. When he wasn't in bed, he was confined to a wheelchair. One sunny day his mother wheeled him out into the yard to get some fresh air. This day, instead of sitting there, he threw himself from the chair. He pulled himself across the grass, dragging his legs behind him. He worked his way to the white picket fence bordering their lot. With great effort, he raised himself up on the fence. Then, stake by stake, he began dragging himself along the fence, resolved that he would walk. He started to do this every day beside the fence. There was nothing he wanted more than to develop life in those legs.

Through daily massages, the boy's iron persistence and his resolute determination, he did develop the ability to stand up, then to walk haltingly, then to walk by himself–and then–to run. He began to walk to school, then run to school, to run for the sheer joy of running. Later in college he made the track team. Still later in Madison Square Garden this young man who was not expected to survive, who would surely never walk, who could never hope to run–this determined young man, Dr. Glenn Cunningham, ran the world's fastest mile![4]

wow!

Here's a checklist for you to ask yourself, to see if what you've settled in your heart-edge also has a passionate edge.

Do I ...

- have a commitment to be continually hungry for more of God in my life and ministry?
- choose friends who share my values and heart and who will press me toward spiritual passion, not suck it out of me?
- hold to a commitment never to be satisfied with just enough–or with success by man's definition, but feel a passion to embrace a dimension of God's calling for me that requires His abundant provision?
- choose to fellowship with other partners in ministry and be edified and challenged?
- choose to keep on growing and learning even when I want to stop?
- keep a commitment to "finish well"–to run the entire race?

1 Samuel 30:6 "David encouraged himself in the Lord."

You cannot maintain a sharper edge unless you're willing to interact with others at the "meeting times" of life.

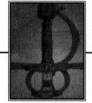

"Not forsaking the assembling of ourselves together."
Hebrews 10:25

ELEVEN

A HIDDEN EDGE

Consider this: You cannot maintain a sharper edge unless you're willing to interact with others at the "meeting times" of life.

It's a tight game. Both teams are battling to win. Each looks for something that will give them the edge over the other. In the end, the home team triumphs. You assess the strengths and weaknesses of both teams and find that everything was pretty much equal. But you were there, and you sensed the edge the home team had. In fact, you probably participated in it. It was more than the home team playing on familiar turf–it was the crowd. The edge was provided by people who never got into the game–at least they didn't pitch or hit or score any runs, but they contributed the "extra" that caused the home team to win. This is the power of presence.

We've all seen it work. We've experienced the difference between an auditorium filled with people versus one where the people are scattered all over. Sociologists use different words to describe and define this phenomenon, but the fact is that beyond all the human reasoning and strategies on the aura of a crowd, there is a vital principle the Bible teaches:

"And let us consider one another in order to stir up love and good works, not forsaking the assembling of ourselves together, as is the manner of some, but exhorting one another, and so much the more as you see the Day approaching."[1]

In our day there is a lack of understanding of the power and dynamic of what God placed in each of us that extends to others in the context of gathering together.

We fall prey to the notion that unless everyone has a part in some physical way, such as speaking or singing, they become only spectators, contributing nothing. I would suggest that God knew the physical limitations that would prohibit individual involvement by everyone in a larger gathering. And that He was thinking of them when the Holy Spirit inspired the words in Hebrews to "forsake not assembling." If so, then there must be a powerful dynamic I bring to a gathering simply by my involved presence.

We are so consumed in our day with individual achievement and visibility that we often miss the foundation of "body ministry." Some parts of our physical bodies will never have visibility, yet they are critical to our lives. Paul brings out this powerful truth in likening the Church to Christ's Body. This is a "hidden" edge.

Likewise, Christians who don't see the value of their presence when the Body gathers shortchange the purpose of God that will be affected that day by their participatory presence.

The bottom line is this–I am important to the gathering of believers whether I ever do anything publicly or not. My involved presence, joined with everyone else, brings a dynamic, a hidden edge, to me and to the meeting that would not be there without my involved presence.

A close friend of mine, Doug Stringer, was invited to attend an important meeting in Washington, D.C. concerning faith-based initiatives. Of mixed heritage, Doug is considered an ethnic minority, so he is often invited, and perhaps as often "used," just on the basis of his ethnicity. He struggled with whether he should take time to attend the meeting, and asked a Washington "insider" his opinion. This man told Doug, "You have to go. You know who makes the decisions in Washington? Whoever shows up. If you don't go, you don't know who will show up, and then you'll be stuck with his decisions, not yours." Doug went.

I believe Christians often lose out by not "showing up" in the meeting times of life, and end up complaining about the decisions that were made. We must become hot–absolutely on fire–with the realization of how important our voice and our vote are.

Talk about living on the edge, look at what one vote has accomplished historically. (These statistics have been published by others elsewhere, but they bear repeating.) For example, Oliver Cromwell won control of England in 1645, when Parliament voted 91 to 90 in his favor. King Charles I was beheaded on the basis of the judges' vote of 68 to 67. France changed from a monarchy to a republic in 1875. The vote of the deputies was 353 to 352.

During the American Revolution, anti-British sentiment was high in many colonies. A bill was presented to the Continental Congress which would have abolished English as the official American language in favor of German. The bill was defeated by one vote. In 1845, the Senate voted 26 to 25 to admit Texas to the union. Indiana's Senator Hannigan changed his mind and voted in favor of its admission. And the senator himself had won his election to office by only one vote.

President Andrew Johnson escaped impeachment in 1868 by one vote. Rutherford B. Hayes was elected President of the United States in 1876 by an electoral vote of 185 to 184.

One candidate for public office in our area recently told me that only 19% of Christians vote. What a tragedy! The ability to determine the outcome of almost any election lies with the Christian community. We seem to be far better at railing against a politician's position after the election than we are at putting people in office who follow Godly, moral principles.

We are living in a crucial day. Moral and economic issues face our law makers that will determine the kind of future we will have as a nation. The decisions of those we elect will determine whether we return to our Godly moral heritage or continue down a pathway that will result ultimately in God's judgment. You can make a difference!

Apathy in the Christian community would vanish if we became personally involved and stopped hiding behind a shield of supposed neutrality. I have no right to lambaste the condition of our nation or its leadership if I am doing nothing to change it for the better. So, let's speak up and get involved and see the moral decay of our nation turn around and "God" put back into our society.

Rev. Martin Neimoller said, "In Germany, they came first for the Communists, and I didn't speak up because I wasn't a Communist. Then they came for the Jews, and I didn't speak up because I wasn't a Jew. Then they came for the trade unionists, and I didn't speak up because I wasn't a trade unionist. Then they came for the Catholics, and I didn't speak up because I was a Protestant. Then they came for me, and by that time no one was left to speak up."

Let's show up for the meeting times of life.

Let's hone our hidden edges!

From
glory to glory–
it's all about
pouring.

"But we all, with unveiled face,
beholding as in a mirror the glory of
the Lord, are being transformed into the same
image from glory to glory,
just as by the Spirit of the Lord."
II Cor 3:18

TWELVE

RIM OF THE CUP

You may have seen an Internet list of "Signs You Worked During the 1990's." Living in the Houston area–home to Enron, the oil industry and NASA, and "Mecca" for engineers–some of my favorites on the list distributed were:

You've sat at the same desk for 4 years and worked for 3 different organizations.

Your resume is in a diskette in your pocket.

You learn about your layoff on the news.

"Vacation" is something you roll over to next year, or a check you get every January.

Your relatives and family describe your job as "working with computers."

Your business cards are no longer correct just one month after you receive them.

You have no hobbies that do not involve an electronic device.

You must fill in your own job performance evaluations and target goals because no one else really knows what you do anyway. Besides, the HR Department was outsourced last month.

Your biggest loss from a system crash is that you've lost your best jokes.

You read this entire list and understood it.

Some of these are sure to hit home, yet they make for a dry, tedious or highly stressful employment existence. Unlike the vicissitudes of life in Corporate America, and even in Entrepreneurial America or Christian Ministry America, our walk with the Lord should keep strengthening, our spirit

[Handwritten marginal notes:
Travel from glory to glory instead of homesteading at the 1st place of glory!
His mercies are new every morning & it is only through our travels w/ Him that we go from glory to glory.]

expanding, our vision fulfilling, our successes piling up, our faith building. That's what we're promised when we live on the edge.

"But we all, with unveiled face, beholding as in a mirror the glory of the Lord, are being transformed into the same image from glory to glory, just as by the Spirit of the Lord."[1]

What kind of spiritual changes have taken place in your life recently? Many Christians never change in the sense of Paul's words to the Corinthians. We might get to "glory" once, but we don't all travel from "glory to glory." Yet, that's exactly what God has for us.

We are all aware of what happens to our bodies when we continue to eat but never exercise. The same thing can be true spiritually because of many Christians feeling pressured to live behind the façade of "having it all together." They continue to input information, but it never becomes knowledge in the sense of a practical application in them, and their only "gain" is just more spiritual weight.

What about you? What will you be next week, next year, or even ten years from now?

Howard Hendricks said, "I have never met a Christian who sat down and planned to live a mediocre life."

When God wants to drill a man, and thrill a man, and skill a man,
When God wants to mold a man
To play for Him the noblest part,
When He yearns with all His heart
To build so great and bold a man
That all the world shall be amazed,
Then watch God's methods, watch His ways!
How He ruthlessly perfects

Whom He royally elects;
How He hammers him and hurts him
And with mighty blows converts him,
Making shapes and forms which only
God Himself can understand,
Even while His man is crying,
Lifting a beseeching hand …
Yet God bends but never breaks
When man's good He undertakes;
When He uses whom He chooses,
And with every purpose fuses
Man to act, and act to man,
As it was when He began,
When God tries His splendor out,
Man will know what He's about![2]

Others have noted, "We really aren't so much human beings as human becomings." There is an ongoing process of becoming the person we will be.

Regardless of the uniqueness of our ministry gifts, God's intention is the same for everyone in the overall sense–to produce in us the character and ministry–the fruit of the Spirit and gifts of the Spirit–of Jesus.[3]

The process is called *transformation*–continual change that produces the fragrance of Christ.

"For we are to God the fragrance of Christ among those who are being saved and among those who are perishing. To the one we are the aroma of death leading to death, and to the other the aroma of life leading to life. And who is sufficient for these things?"[4]

One day missionary Amy Carmichael, who devoted her life to rescuing girls who had been dedicated to a life of slavery and shame in an Indian Hindu Temple, took some of her children to see a goldsmith refining gold in the ancient manner of the Orient. The man sat beside a small charcoal fire. On top of the coals lay a common red curved roof-tile, and another tile over it like a lid. This was his homemade crucible. The man had a mixture of salt, tamarind fruit, and burnt brick dust that he called his "medicine" for the purifying of the gold. He dropped a lump of ore into the blistering mixture and let the fire "eat it." After a while, the man lifted the gold out with a pair of tongs, let it cool, and studied it. Then he replaced the gold in the crucible and blew the fire hotter than it was before. This process went on and on, the fire growing hotter and hotter.

"The gold could not bear it so hot at first," explained the goldsmith, "but it can bear it now—what would have destroyed it helped it."

As the children watched the gold being purified in the fire, someone asked the man, "How do you know when the gold is purified?"

The man's answer: "When I can see my face in it (the liquid gold in the crucible), then it is pure."5

Jeremiah illustrated this process of growth and why it was needed, by comparing the nation of Moab to a wine being created.

"Moab has been at ease from his youth; he has settled on his dregs, and has not been emptied from vessel to vessel, nor has he gone into captivity. Therefore his taste remained in him, and his scent has not changed."6 Jer. 48

The pouring from "vessel to vessel" separates the pure fruit of the vine from the dregs. Dregs are anything that taint your life and give a bitter quality to you.

Consider these observations in this illustration:
1. If not separated from the dregs, they will ultimately destroy the intent of the wine by making it bitter. Regardless of how gifted I am, dregs, if not separated from my life, will destroy the purpose of God in me.
2. The pouring always makes waves. You can't be poured from vessel to vessel without being at least somewhat unsettled.
3. The containers of life are different sizes and shapes, but they produce Christlikeness. "And we know all things [good and bad] work together for good to those who love God, to those who are the called according to His purpose."[7] Why? "... That I might be conformed to Christ."[8]

Pouring produces a newness. Notice the words "new scent," "new fragrance," "new taste" in the previous verses. As we are poured, we are "transformed" from "glory to glory." Pouring is a choice. A good choice. Is the rim of your cup dry? Or is the edge moistened from being poured, ready to pour again?

"But we all, with unveiled face, beholding as in a mirror the glory of the Lord, are being transformed into the same image from glory to glory, just as by the Spirit of the Lord."[9]

Without a
marriage that works,
ministry and
even careers seem
hollow and superficial
at best.

"Love will cover a
multitude of sins."
I Peter 4:8

THIRTEEN

AN EDGE CALLED FIDELITY

Becky and I have been married more than three decades–and we've spent all of those years in vocational ministry. At 19 and 20 years of age, we were babes toddling off on a journey called life, knowing little about marriage and less about the challenges we would face in marriage and ministry. God has been gracious to us, though, and through the years and the struggles, we've learned some valuable lessons, our lives truly being joined together.

In this day, when relationships are crashing all around us, we need some foundational principles and priorities on which to build solid marriages and ministries. My observation is that without a marriage that works, ministry and even careers are hollow and superficial at best.

More often than not, when the marriage relationship isn't working, the resulting cover-up produces a Christian message that is only proclaimed, but not lived. A healthy marriage isn't free from disagreements and painful adjustments that are difficult to resolve. But when a marriage is working, there is a healthy sense of admiration, honor, trust, and growth that helps navigate such difficulties.

A man and his wife were having some problems at home and were giving each other the silent treatment. The next week the man realized that he would need his wife to wake him at 5:00 a.m. for an early morning business flight to Chicago. Not wanting to be the first to break the silence (and lose), he wrote on a piece of paper, "Please wake me at 5:00 a.m." The next morning the man woke up, only to discover it was 9:00 a.m. and that he had missed his flight. Furious, he was about to go and see why his wife hadn't awakened him when he noticed a piece of paper by the bed. The paper said, "It is 5:00 a.m. Wake up." I've discovered that men just aren't equipped for these sorts of contests!

I want to walk you through some of what Becky and I have learned during our thirty plus years together.

Setting Boundaries that are Never Violated

No couple can afford *not* to set boundaries as they go along. They need to be set in concrete and *never* violated. What boundaries have you established toward members of the opposite sex you counsel or work with? What are the safeguards that will help you avoid the "very appearance of evil"? What do you do when there is even the hint of temptation sexually?

Keeping Romance in Marriage

Ricky, age 10, was asked, "How would you make a marriage work?" He said, "Tell your wife that she looks pretty even if she looks like a truck."

What do you do to keep the sizzle in your relationship? Marriages tend to become mundane. Little things like cards, flowers, gifts, dinners, spontaneous ways of expressing and affirming worth keep the romance in your relationship.

Becky always wanted to go to Hawaii, but it seemed as if there wasn't much money for extras like that. One year, however, I saved enough money to take her to Hawaii–but she didn't know. A friend of ours, Sharon Adams, was going over to meet her husband at the end of one of his ministry trips and

Becky had been saying for a long time–I wish we could afford to go to Hawaii. I just played along. I had Sharon pack Becky's suitcase because we were taking Sharon to the airport. When we arrived at the airport we walked Sharon to the gate. All of the time Becky is going on and on about how she wished she could go to Hawaii. I, of course, did everything I could to pour it on. When it came time to board we walked over to the gate and there I handed Becky a Hawaii tourist bag and she discovered that she and I were going, too. We still laugh about the "before" Becky–when it was always someone else who got to go–and the "after" Becky who was like a kid in a candy shop.

Raising Children Together

Derrick, age 8, was asked–How can a stranger tell if two people are married? His answer, "You might have to guess, based on whether they seem to be yelling at the same kids."

There is nothing like children either to draw two people closer together or to begin building a divisive wedge. Where to draw the line in discipline is often the area of the most contention and strife. As a father or mother, your example in your love for God, love for your spouse, your personal integrity, your humanness (no plastic faces), admitting when you are wrong and asking forgiveness not only develop children who are well-balanced spiritually and emotionally, but also deepen and strengthen the marriage relationship.

Reserving Time for Intimacy

Intimacy means more than your sexual relationship. I was stunned many years ago when Becky informed me that I really didn't know her or know anything about women. I'd like to say that my response was Christlike–filled with gentleness and humility. The truth is that I proceeded to defend myself and inform her of how qualified I was to know because of people who listened to me in ministry.

That was a huge mistake. I obviously hadn't been married long enough to learn the following key words and their meanings.

Someone wrote, "what I have learned after 25 years of marriage..."

1. FINE–This is the word a woman uses at the end of any argument that she feels she is right about, but needs to shut you up. NEVER use "fine" to describe how a woman looks. This will cause you to have one of those arguments.

2. FIVE MINUTES–This is half an hour. It is equivalent to the five minutes that your football/baseball or whatever game is going to last before you take out the trash, so she feels that it's an even trade.

3. NOTHING–This means something and you should be on your toes. "Nothing" is usually used to describe the feeling a woman has of wanting to turn you inside out, upside down, and backwards. "Nothing" usually signifies an argument that will last "FIVE MINUTES" and end with the word "FINE."

4. GO AHEAD (with raised eyebrows)–This is a dare. One that will result in a woman getting upset over "nothing" and eventually cause an argument that will last "five minutes."

5. GO AHEAD (without raised eyebrows)–This means "I give up. Do what you want because I don't care."

You will, however, get a Raised Eyebrow "Go Ahead" in just a few minutes, followed by "Nothing," and a "Five Minute" argument ending with "Fine."

6. LOUD SIGH–Not actually a word of course but often a verbal cue misunderstood by men. The "Loud Sigh" means she thinks you're an idiot and wonders why she is wasting her time standing there having a "Five Minute" argument with you over "Nothing."

7. OH–This word followed by any statement is trouble, e.g., "Oh, let me get that," which actually means you are obviously incapable and incompetent and cannot possibly complete the task to her particular standard.

My response to Becky seemed to mean nothing to her. She quickly informed me that she didn't care how many people I ministered to–I still knew nothing about women.

On top of that, she bought me a book on understanding women and wanted me to read it. When the Lord finished working me over, I acknowledged to her how right she was. I read the book. It not only gave me the right perspective of how women react and think, but healed an area of our marriage that I always assumed was Becky's fault. I was to blame all along and couldn't see it. Knowing the other person in a relationship takes time to talk, to share, to dream, to really bond. There is no substitute.

Partners Together in Ministry

I don't have a ministry without Becky. Perhaps most people sitting in the pew listening to me would find that hard to believe. Becky will probably never be a preacher. She does not want to be one. She is, however, as equally important to our assignment in ministry as I am. Ministry is a partnership!

Over the years, I have watched Becky work through insecurities and fears and take more of a leading role, allowing God to use her in ways that are outside her comfort zone. Her development in ministry is one of the most fulfilling things of my life. I share equally in her accomplishments.

By encouraging my development in ministry and putting confidence in me—many times far greater than my own—Becky has helped me to become far more than I ever imagined. Covering weakness is as important as encouraging growth. Peter says, "Love will cover a multitude of sins."[1]

Thank God for spouses who love us in spite of our flaws!

Serving, Submitting, and Cherishing

These three words are the core of any vital marriage. Imperfect people have learned to serve each other, submit to each other, and cherish each other. My nature is to control. For years I practiced that in our marriage. But slowly and painfully, I have learned and am still learning that true leadership descends to the basin and towel rather than ascending to a self-made throne. Jesus preached to the thousands, healed them, fed them, but He also washed the disciples' feet. When you take the towel, it is amazing how people you're called to lead, even your wife and family, will respond.

Thirty years and still learning, on our way in the journey called life ... Thirty years and still grateful God put Becky in my life ... Thirty years and something still happens in me when I see her across the room ... Thirty years and a wonderful wife who has stuck by me through thick and thin—two daughters and sons-in-law who love Jesus and us, too–and four grandchildren who are the smartest, best-looking, and most gifted you've ever seen!

To miss your inheritance would be tragic.

"I pray … the eyes of your
understanding being enlightened …
what are the riches of
the glory of
His inheritance in the Saints."
Ephesians 1:18

FOURTEEN

THE EDGE OF HOLINESS

We seem to be quite good at making our call to be holy people mean either a very legalistic set of values and regulations or to dismiss any practical outworking of holiness affecting our lifestyle as only positional in Christ. Yet it was a true Holy Spirit encounter that impacted my life in a dramatic way.

It was the middle of the night. I heard these words deep in my spirit–"the tithe is holy to me." I knew it wasn't too much pizza because I've had the Lord deal with me in similar fashion many times during my almost thirty years of pastoring. However, I wasn't sure exactly what the Lord was trying to speak to me. I knew what Leviticus 27 says, but I sensed it was more than that.

This incident began a period of several days in which I progressively understood God's message to me. I sensed the Lord telling me that there are things He has called "holy" or placed high importance on that we in our day look at as options. Our thinking seems to be, "If I feel like it, I'll do it–be a part, show up, live like that, etc., but if I don't feel like it–No Big Deal!" And because we live with that mentality we miss what He has purposed for our lives. The next day during my devotion time I read Hebrews 12 "… or profane person like Esau who for one morsel of food sold his birthright."

I've read through the book of Hebrews many times–even preached through it as a message series, but didn't remember this verse. It jumped out at me. I remember thinking–I would call Esau a fool. It's a dumb thing to sell your birthright for a bowl of soup, but I'm not sure I would call him profane.

That word really intrigued me. What did it mean? I went

to the dictionary and discovered that it means literally–"before the temple." Some of the definitions were: "Not sacred, not hallowed, or consecrated, showing disrespect or contempt for sacred things–things made common." The word used in the New Testament means "permitted to be trodden."

Suppose you owned a very expensive jacket made by the best and most creative designer in the world. The materials used were hand-picked and of the finest quality. Let's say you paid several thousand dollars for your jacket. How would you feel if I came over to you, took your jacket, threw it on the floor and began to walk all over it?

After I researched the word profane, that was the picture that came to me. Esau profaned his birthright (his inheritance). He treated it like it was common, no big deal. In a sense he walked all over it. I then understood that God was showing me that we do the same thing when we treat the things He calls holy as though they are unimportant.

Holy has to do with something set apart, highly valued, separated from the rest for a destined purpose.

Over the next few days the Lord brought one thing after another to my mind from the Bible that He calls holy or places high value on. I understood that when we ignore these issues in our lives we forfeit something of ever living out His inheritance in us. When Esau sold his birthright he gave up his destiny.

The sons were seated at a meal in the order of their birth. It was through the first-born that the family line was confirmed. The first-born received double the inheritance of the rest of the children. The first-born was given the kingdom as his right. Whatever the domain of rulership the father had, the first-born son received. When we choose to become a Christ-follower, the Bible says that "to as many as received

Him to them He gives the power to become sons of God."[1] The interesting thing with God is that we are called "first" sons with a birthright inheritance in God that if we are not careful, we won't ever comprehend, much less live in.

"Therefore I also, after I heard of your faith in the Lord Jesus and your love for all the saints, do not cease to give thanks for you, making mention of you in my prayers: that the God of our Lord Jesus Christ, the Father of glory, may give to you the spirit of wisdom and revelation in the knowledge of Him, the eyes of your understanding being enlightened; that you may know what is the hope of His calling, what are the riches of the glory of His inheritance in the saints."[2]

Paul's concern is that the Ephesian Christians would miss what was their inheritance in Christ. As the Lord brought to mind each of these things He places high value on, I realized that my treating them as common, as it were, walking all over them, no big deal–optional–could keep me from the benefits of "His" inheritance in me.

For example, take the first one the Lord dealt with me about. The tithe (tenth) is holy to me.[3] Immediately our red flags go up. Old Testament law–we're now under grace. However, let me suggest that the real issue here is not "law," but "firstness." It is about the fruit of men's labor and the tangible expression of first place worship. When God speaks of the tithe (tenth) and the subsequent benefits to all who obey, He talks about it in the context of sowing, reaping, and harvest.[4] When He deals with the subject of New Testament giving, it is in the context of harvest–sowing and reaping.[5] You cannot reap at a different dimension than you sow. In each case the Lord says, "I will supply abundantly"–Old Testament–"open windows of heaven and pour out." New Testament–"multiply the seed you have sown."

1 Co 9:8—?.

Part of our inheritance is abundant provision for every good work.[6] Most are unaware of just how much Jesus talked about money. Not because money is important to God, but rather it's important to us. Jesus made a very powerful statement, "Therefore if you have not been faithful in the unrighteous mammon, who will commit to your trust the true riches?"[7]

"Mammon" is the word for money and what money can buy. Without elaborating further, Jesus' call to us is two-fold: 1) To be worshippers–to give Him first place worship in all we do, all we are, and all we have. 2) To be effective and wise managers of everything He places into our hands. How powerful are these words–if you can't be trusted with money and what money can buy, will God trust you with the true spiritual riches of the Kingdom–which money cannot buy? Obviously not. I believe the "true riches" have to do with our inheritance in Christ where we experience His power towards us who believe according to the working of His mighty power.[8]

According to Jesus, the release of His power is tied to how we handle our money at least to some degree. The point is–how many people who love God miss out on the part of their inheritance in Christ where His power is brought to bear on the human scene in ministry that releases the captive, imparts transforming life, and speaks healing into human suffering–ministry that is beyond human resources, but not beyond God's power.

It continually amazes me that good people who love the Lord live with a poverty mentality believing that everything of life's supply is up to them. Those who do will never know what it means to be entrusted with the "true riches" of the Kingdom.

Early in our marriage, Becky and I would face this issue: Would we live with a grasping closed hand that wouldn't release our resources or would we live open handed allowing the Lord to flow through us in abundance where by faith we trusted Him for our provision?

I remember vividly the period of time the Lord was dealing with me to trust Him for our provision by giving the first ten percent of our income to Him. In our case, we couldn't afford to tithe. We had bills left over after the money ran out as it was. One day at noon I went home for lunch and told Becky–"We're going to start tithing. I want you to pay our tithes first even if we can't pay our bills. We are going to trust God."

We had way more credit than we could handle. We had purchased a sofa and love seat that we were sure would really make us somebody. It's amazing what you think will contribute to your self worth. We made a commitment that we would never again buy furniture on credit and that we would not buy any more furniture until the sofa and love seat were completely paid off and we had money for something new. By the time that happened the furniture had actually changed colors because we had worn enough of the finish off the material to reveal what was underneath.

During that season we learned to manage what was placed into our hands and we learned to honor God with the firstfruits of our increase. Today we give many times over ten percent and God keeps giving it back in abundance. But far more important than that is the dimension of ministry the Lord has entrusted to us. When Becky and I began in ministry, our life's goal was to pastor a church of 200. That seemed impossible to us. Today we minister to thousands of people every week in our worship gatherings, many more by television across our nation and I head an international fellowship of churches.

Watching God display His power in shaping and changing lives and ministering wholeness at every point of human need, I stand in awe at the power of His "true riches." How grateful I am that in a tiny apartment in Modesto, California at our noonday meal we decided to honor what God calls "holy" and as a result entered into His inheritance in us.

As we consider
our lack in the light of His
greatness, we move to a
position of trust and then
to risk.

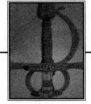

"With God all things are possible."
Matthew 19:26

FIFTEEN

RAZOR'S EDGE LIVING

Major corporations laying off thousands of workers ... companies failing ... the national debt out of control and beyond the ability of our elected leaders to do anything about reducing it ... the economy in shambles ... the world unstable with the future uncertain ... all signs of our time and the seeds that breed a growing pessimism in the hearts and minds of people.

This malaise hits and soon you can hear it in how people talk–a subtle hopelessness. If the circumstances of our day forecast a hopeless present and future, we–who are mature, we of spiritual leadership, we with the sharpened edge–are faced with a choice. If we are not discerning and choose well, we will fall prey to a Satanic ploy that causes us to believe that the situation is only what we can see and perceive in the natural, and the only resources we have are those we can count.

"But the men who had gone up with him said, 'We are not able to go up against the people, for they are stronger than we.' And they gave the children of Israel a bad report of the land which they had spied out, saying, 'The land through which we have gone as spies is a land that devours its inhabitants, and all the people whom we saw in it are men of great stature. There we saw the giants (the descendants of Anak came from the giants); and we were like grasshoppers IN OUR OWN SIGHT, and so we were in their sight.' "[1]

Anytime you begin to look at the challenge God puts in front of you through *your own sight*, fear will turn faith into feelings and then feelings will cause failure to accomplish the task. Not only will you not take the challenge, but those around you that you influence will also be struck with fear and will retreat from the task at hand. "So all the congregation lifted up their voices and cried, and the people wept that night."[2] When we succumb to this mindset, there is a paralysis that sets in to cripple every dimension of Kingdom advancement.

Our hope is not in our economy, our government, labor statistics, or the rise and fall of companies, stocks or nations–our hope is in our God who specializes in bringing hope and harvest in hopeless and barren times.

God will do great things in the midst of difficult days, while things fail in which people have put their trust. Engineers trust their calculators, investors trust their stock forecasting, and pilots trust their instruments–but only the Word of God is infallible.

Years ago, billionaire H. Ross Perot gave his son a stack of papers with everything on it that Perot Sr. knew about business. He later added to it and published it as a book. In it, Perot told his son that at every minute, their business was on the razor's edge of success or failure.

In the same way, you experience razor's edge living minute by minute as you turn your focus toward earth or toward Heaven, faith, and God's perspective. What is your outlook? Are you seeing only the problems of our day? Or do you see the great possibilities that exist? Our hope is never in the tangible things of this world that will rust and decay and even pass away. Our hope is in the One who upholds the entire universe by the Word of His power.[3]

The antidote to the fears and pressures of this world is to walk by faith, with trust and reliance upon the Lord. But take it a step further–before faith, there must be something for which we trust Him. An impossible moment filled with fear.

Frustration. Discouragement. Stress. The overwhelming possibility of failure. Facing these, God then begins to show us that where we are inadequate, He is more than able. As we consider our lack in the light of His greatness, we move to a position of trust, and then to risk.

This process not only begins any large step of faith in our lives, but it continues throughout the project. Walking by faith is exactly that–a journey. It is daily, active, ongoing razor's edge living.

"No pain no gain," some say. I have to admit I'm far more interested in the gain than I am the pain. Still, I know that few accomplishments in life are achieved without a price.

History is filled with people who trumphed in spite of their handicaps.

"Cripple him, and you have a Sir Walter Scott.

"Lock him in a prison cell, and you have a John Bunyan.

"Bury him in the snows of Valley Forge, and you have a George Washington.

"Raise him in abject poverty, and you have an Abraham Lincoln.

"Subject him to bitter religious prejudice and you have a Disraeli.

"Strike him down with infantile paralysis and he becomes a Franklin D. Roosevelt.

"Burn him so severely in a schoolhouse fire that the doctors say he will never walk again, and you have a Glenn Cunningham who set the world's record in 1934 for running a mile in four minutes and 6.7 seconds. p.74-75

"Deafen a genius composer, and you have a Ludwig van Beethoven.

"Have him or her born black in a society filled with racial

Death of Esther's parents + captivity of Jews led her to become queen + save her people

Many abused women teach out of the depth of comfort + restoration + freedom they received out of the cross

Diving accident - Joni Erikson Tada

discrimination, and you have a Booker T. Washington, a George Washington Carver, or a Martin Luther King, Jr.

"Make him the first child to survive a Nazi concentration camp, paralyze him from the waist down when he is four, and you have incomparable concert violinist, Itzhak Perlman.

"Call him a slow learner, 'retarded,' and write him off as uneducable, and you have an Albert Einstein."[4]

As much as it may hurt to go through it, we're far better off with the pain than many people who never start because of fear, frustration, discouragement, stress, or failure. Many who begin soon quit because they encounter some of those same obstacles along the way and begin to wonder if they ever heard from God in the first place.

The same Lord who places within our hearts the faith to embrace His vision will also meet us at each crisis moment along the way. Remember, the pain–the struggle that comes from seeing our lack of resource–always comes before the gain–which is the heart assurance that God is more than able, He is mighty to see you through, and faithful to do for you that which He has done for others. God will always provide exactly what you need to accomplish His intended purpose.

Blake is my oldest grandson. His third grade teacher related the following story to his mother. Every student had to say in front of the class the portion of scripture they were required to memorize for that week. When it came one of the boy's turn he began to cry because he couldn't remember the verse. Blake got out of his seat, walked around the classroom, put his arm around the boy, knelt down beside him and said, "You can do this. Let me tell you what I do when I haven't memorized my verse. I let everyone else go before me and I listen and keep repeating it over and over until it is my turn. By the time everyone else has said it, I have repeated it so many times, I can say it."

The teacher watched all of this happen and told Blake's Mom, "Even if the boy had gotten it wrong, I would have passed him." It's God who puts His arm around us, encourages us, shows us how, and then rejoices in "passing us" in the challenges of life.

So, whether it's God's vision of feeding a city, building a building, taking a new position or whatever He calls you to–GO AHEAD–ask the Lord to show you His intended purpose for your life! Work through the pain of it being too big, too hard, impossible for you but not for Him.

When we near the end of life's race, may each of us be able to say with Paul, "I have fought the good fight, I have finished the race, I have kept the faith. Finally, there is laid up for me the crown of righteousness, which the Lord, the righteous Judge, will give to me on that Day, and not to me only but also to all who have loved His appearing."4

Let's sharpen our edges and finish well!

NOTES

Chapter 1
[1] Alfred A. Montapert

Chapter 2
[1] Philippians 3:13b
[2] Ecclesiastes 11:4-6 NKJV
[3] Genesis 26:1-12

Chapter 3
[1] John 6:5-9 NKJV
[2] Acts 10:38
[3] 1 John 3:8

Chapter 4
[1] Philippians 3:20 NKJV
[2] Philippians 3:18-19 NKJV
[3] Katherine Fullerton Gerould
[4] John Hagee, *How to Win Over Worry,* Harvest House Publishers, 1987
[5] Helen Mallicoat, quoted in Tim Hansel, *Holy Sweat,* Thomas Nelson, 1989
[6] Mark 10:27
[7] Romans 8:37
[8] Philippians 4:13 NKJV
[9] Philippians 3:13-14 NKJV

Chapter 5
[1] Beloit College, Wisconsin
[2] Revelation 12:11a
[3] Lamentations 3:23
[4] Philippians 3:12 NKJV

Chapter 6
[1] Alan Redpath, *Victorious Christian Service Studies in Nehemiah*

Chapter 7
[1] Philippians 3:13-14
[2] Douglas Adams, *Last Chance to See,* Ballantine, 1990
[3] Matthew 23:27 NKJV

Chapter 8
[1] Micah 6:8 NKJV
[2] Psalm 133:1 NKJV
[3] John 13:35 NKJV
[4] Romans 12:15 NKJV

Chapter 9
[1] Christianity Today Magazine, July, 1991
[2] Webster's New World Dictionary of the American Language College Edition, Simon & Schuster

[3] 1 Corinthians 12:18-20 NKJV
[4] 2 Corinthians 5:15, 17
[5] Proverbs 6:16-19 NKJV
[6] James 3:8-12 KJV
[7] 1 Corinthians 12:4-27
[8] 1 Corinthians 11:29-30
[9] Ephesians 4:1-7 NKJV

Chapter 10
[1] David A. Berman, *Chicken Soup for the Soul,* HCI Publishers, 1993
[2] Philippians 3:15 NKJV
[3] 2 Timothy 1:6 NKJV
[4] Burt Dubin, Personal Achievement Institute Burt@speakingBizSuccess.com

Chapter 11
[1] Hebrews 10:24, 25 NKJV

Chapter 12
[1] 2 Corinthians 3:18 NKJV
[2] Dale Martin Stone, *Sourcebook of Poetry*
[3] 1 Corinthians 12:4, 5
[4] 2 Corinthians 2:15-16 NKJV
[5] Robert Wise, *When There is No Miracle*, Hearthstone Publishing Company, 1998
[6] Jeremiah 48:11 NKJV —ịↄ l-20
[7] Romans 8:28 NKJV (brackets mine)
[8] Romans 8:29 NKJV
[9] 2 Corinthians 3:18 NKJV

Chapter 13
[1] Peter 4:8 AMP

Chapter 14
[1] John 1:12
[2] Ephesians 1:15-18 NKJV
[3] Leviticus 27:32 AMP
[4] Malachi 3
[5] 1 Corinthians 9
[6] 1 Corinthians 9:8
[7] Luke 16:11
[8] Ephesians 1:19 NKJV

Chapter 15
[1] Numbers 13:31-33 NKJV
[2] Numbers 14:1 NKJV
[3] Hebrews 1:3 NKJV
[4] Ted Engstrom, *The Pursuit of Excellence,* Daybreak Books, 1982
[5] 2 Timothy 4:7-8 NKJV

Watch for More Watercolor Books®

By terrific authors like

Edwin Louis Cole

Nancy Corbett Cole

Donald Ostrom

G. F. Watkins

Karen Davis

Many more!

www.watercolorbooks.com

Study curriculum available for most books.

Southlake, Texas

Steve Riggle is Senior Pastor and founder of Grace Community Church, a congregation of many thousands located in Houston, Texas. He also serves as the President of the Christian Evangelistic Assemblies, a fellowship of churches throughout the United States and the world. He has served as a senior pastor since the 1970's and has an extensive background in church planting and multiple church-related ministries to the community. He has been married to Becky for over thirty years and has two married daughters, two grandsons, and two granddaughters.

Contact him at:
Grace Community Church
P.O. Box 891409
Houston, TX 77289-1409
www.gracecchouston.org